ZOOM OUT

OUT

NATURAL WORLD

ZOOM OUT

NATURAL WORLD

Illustrated by
OWEN DAVEY

DK

CONTENTS

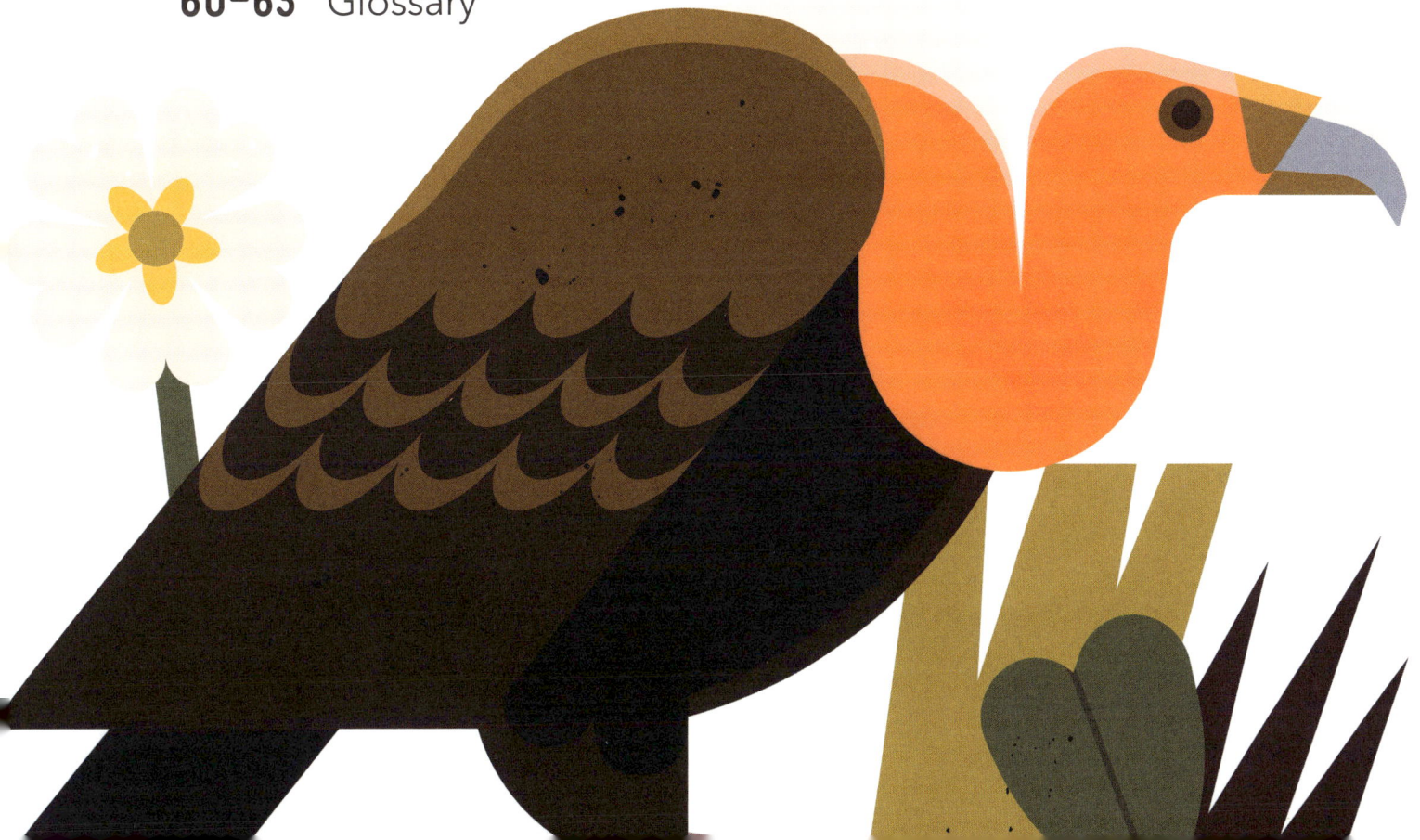

OUR WORLD

Earth is an extraordinary place. Of all the billions of planets spinning through space, ours is the only one that we know of that can support life. The important ingredients of air, light, warmth, water, and food make it possible for an amazing variety of plants and animals, including humans, to grow and multiply.

AIR

A blanket of gases, called the atmosphere, surrounds the Earth, protecting us from the Sun's harmful rays. It contains oxygen, the gas that animals need to survive. Mammals, like us, take in oxygen with lungs, but fish use gills to take oxygen out of the water and some animals, like worms, absorb it through their skin.

SUN

Earth is just the right distance from the Sun to be not too hot and not too cold. It gives us heat and light, which plants need to grow. Plants provide animals and humans with food and shelter. Plants also make oxygen for us to breathe.

WATER

From space our planet looks blue because most of its surface is covered by deep, salty oceans. Only 3 per cent of Earth's water is fresh. It falls as rain and snow and collects in streams, rivers, ponds, and lakes. A lot of water is frozen at the icy North and South Pole and on mountain peaks. Plants and animals need water to stay healthy.

LAND

Thirty per cent of the Earth's surface is land. A layer of soil covers most of the planet. The soil is what feeds us. It holds nutrients and water for trees, plants, and crops to grow. It also provides a home for billions of creatures, from tiny bugs to burrowing bears.

WEATHER AND CLIMATE

Weather starts with the Sun. Without its rays to heat the oceans and warm the air, clouds would not form, rain and snow would not fall, and the wind would not blow. Different parts of the planet have their own patterns of weather, called climates. Climates can be mild, warm, wet, dry, cold, or hot. Every climate zone is home to animals and plants that have adapted to the conditions.

LIVING THINGS

Every inch of our planet is bursting with life. There are 80 billion people who share the space, food, and water with a mind-boggling array of flying, swimming, slithering, and crawling living things. There are around 130 billion mammals, over 400 billion birds, 3.5 trillion fish, and 10 million trillion insects!

HABITATS

Earth's surface is vast and varied, and so are the plants and animals that live on it. Different environments are called habitats and each one provides the shelter, climate, and landscape that suits a particular collection of creatures. A habitat can be anything from a shallow rockpool to a soaring mountain.

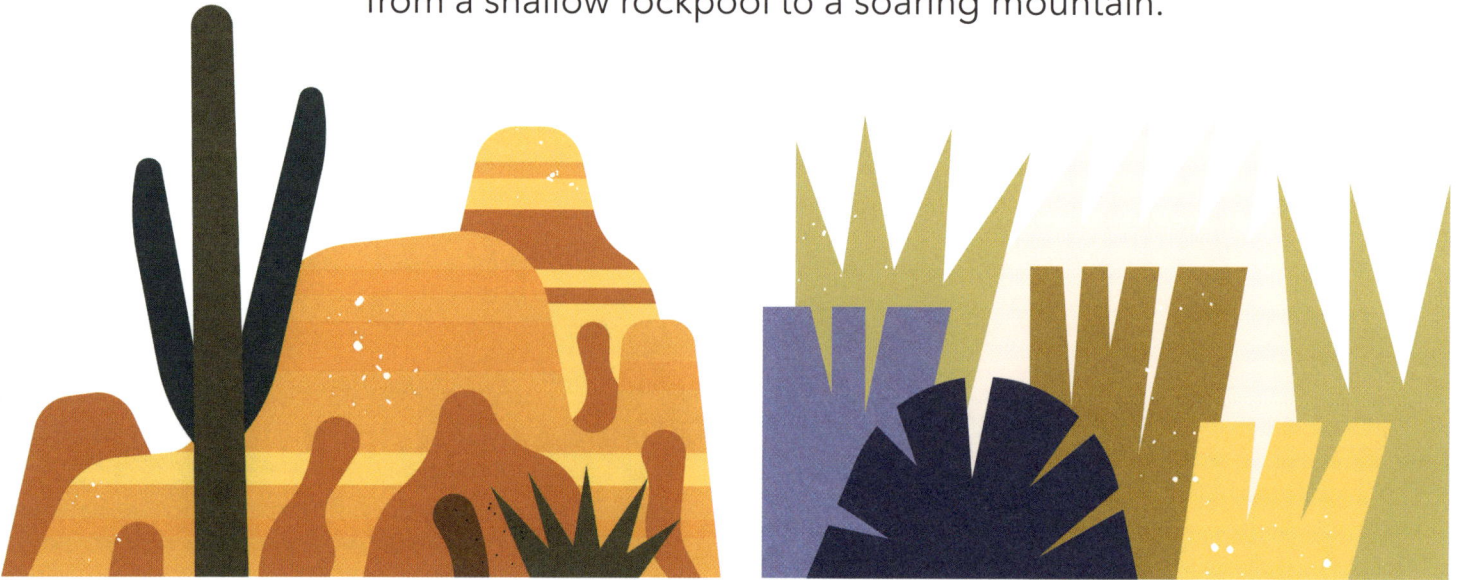

DESERTS

Deserts are hot or cold, but always dry. In hot deserts, animals shelter during the heat of the day and emerge at night. Most get their water from the food they eat. Cold deserts are often found above the clouds on high plateaus. The biggest desert in the world is Antarctica – the ice-covered land at the South Pole where it hardly ever snows.

GRASSLANDS

Grasslands get more rain than deserts, but not enough for trees to grow. Tropical grasslands, such as Africa's savannas, have a wet season and a dry season. They provide food for herds of plant-eaters, which are preyed on by large predators. Temperate grasslands have hot summers and cold winters. They are known as prairies in America and steppe in Europe and Asia.

FORESTS

Forests grow in places where there is plenty of rain. Tropical rainforests are warm and wet all year. Their towering trees provide food and shelter for millions of different animals. Snowy, northern countries have boreal forests of evergreen trees. Temperate forests have warm summers and cool, frosty winters. In cool climates, forest animals survive the winter by storing food or hibernating until the spring.

WOW!
Forests are home to more than 80 per cent of all land-living species of animals, plants, and insects.

MOUNTAINS

The lower slopes of mountains are often covered with lush forests, but their peaks are cold, barren, and steep. Mountain-dwelling animals are adapted to the harsh habitat with thick fur and feet that grip the slopes.

POLAR

The North and South Poles at the top and bottom of the world are freezing cold, but the icy waters teem with life. In the Arctic, polar bears hunt seals on the floating sea ice. In Antarctica, penguins nest on the land and dive off the coast to catch fish.

FRESHWATER

Rain gathers in ponds and lakes or flows back to the sea along rivers and streams. In wetland habitats, water soaks the soil to form marshes and swamps. Freshwater habitats are wildlife hotspots for fish, birds, frogs, snakes, and water-loving mammals such as otters and beavers.

OCEANS

The Pacific, Atlantic, Indian, Arctic, and Southern Oceans wrap around the world. They range from deep and cold, to shallow and warm. There are many different ocean habitats in the water and on the shore, from cliffs and sand dunes to kelp forests and coral reefs.

WHAT IS AN ECOSYSTEM?

An ecosystem is all the animals and plants that exist together in one place. For an ecosystem to stay healthy, it needs a balance of all of its native species as they all depend on each other for survival. Non-living things such as the weather, seasons, water, and soil also play a part in an ecosystem.

Polar bears have two kinds of fur. An outer layer of long, straight, wiry hair gives protection to the inner fur from the water. A soft layer of woolly, wavy fur underneath keeps the bears warm.

ZOOM IN!
Polar bears blend in perfectly with their snowy surroundings, but their fur is not white – it's translucent. Sunlight scatters as each hair reflects the visible light, making them appear white.

Beneath the fur, polar bear skin is black. The dark colour helps the bears absorb more heat from the sun. A four-inch-thick covering of fat under their skin provides warmth and energy.

POLAR BEAR

PATIENT AND POWERFUL, FEARSOME AND FEARLESS

Scientific name: Ursus maritimus | **Lifespan in wild:** 18–25 years | **Height:** 160 cm on four legs, 270 cm on two legs | **Length:** 2–3 m | **Weight:** 150–350 kg (females) 350–650 kg (males) | **Location:** Across the Arctic Ocean in parts of Canada, USA (Alaska), Russia, Greenland, and Norway (Svalbard).

Male polar bears can weigh as much as 10 men. They are the planet's biggest meat-eating land mammals, but they also live on water! Their scientific name means 'sea bear' because they swim in the icy Arctic Ocean and roam across its frozen surface.

LIFE ON THE ICE

The sea ice is where polar bears hunt, rest, travel, and bring up their young. They rely on their senses and strength to capture their main prey – seals. Although they spend half their lives hunting, they only catch one or two seals with every ten attempts.

The bears often wait patiently next to breathing holes. When a seal comes up for air, they grasp the slippery prey with their long, curved claws. Polar bears can sniff out seal pups that are born in dens in the sea ice. They pound through the den's roof to reach the pups.

Polar bears are strong swimmers and travel long distances in search of food. They use their large front paws like paddles to power through the water. They glide silently past islands of floating ice, checking for seals that have hauled up to rest. When they spot their prey, the bears dive below the surface to approach unnoticed.

WOW!
Polar bears can smell their prey up to 32 kilometres away. They can even smell seals beneath thick snow or ice from a kilometre away.

HIDDEN DEPTHS

The Arctic is the most northerly place on the planet. It is almost entirely covered by the Arctic Ocean, which freezes over during the winter. Some parts are covered with ice all year round. Beneath the glistening, white wilderness, the cold water teems with life. It provides food for a variety of creatures, big and small, that all depend on each other to survive.

PLANKTON

Plankton are tiny plants and animals that drift with the ocean currents. Arctic plankton are a nutritious food for swarms of small, shrimp-like creatures, called krill. The krill, in turn, are an important food for fish, seals, and large whales.

ARCTIC COD

Arctic cod can survive the sub-zero temperatures under the sea ice because their blood contains special protein that stops it from freezing. They feed on plankton and krill and grow large enough to make a meal for seals and whales. The cod hide from these hungry predators in cracks in the ice.

SEALS

The Arctic is home to six different species of seal: ribbon seals, bearded seals, ringed seals, spotted seals, harp seals, and hooded seals. They feed on crabs, clams, and fish. Seals' blubber makes them a high-energy food for hungry polar bears and their cubs.

NARWHALS

These strange and beautiful creatures are often called 'the unicorns of the sea' because of their long, spiral tusks. Unlike other whales that are seasonal visitors to the Arctic, narwhals live here all year round, feeding on crabs, squid, and fish.

TIGER

STEALTHY AND SOLITARY, BEAUTIFUL AND STRONG

Scientific name: Panthera tigris | **Lifespan in wild:** up to 15 years
Length: up to 3 m | **Weight:** 100–300 kg | **Location:** Bangladesh,
Bhutan, China, India, Indonesia, Malaysia, Myanmar, Nepal, Russia, and Thailand.

The biggest of all the Asian wild cats can be found in many habitats, from steamy swamps to forests and grasslands. These powerful hunters have no natural enemies. They prowl silently at night, using their excellent eyesight and hearing to track down their prey.

Tigers have a reflective layer at the back of their eyes that acts like a mirror, reflecting light back into the eye and boosting night vision. This feature is what makes tigers' eyes glow in the dark when a light is shone on them.

ZOOM IN!
Tigers' eyes are specially adapted to see in low light. Large pupils let in the maximum amount of light.

SILENT HUNTER

Tigers live and hunt alone. During the day, they usually find a shady spot to sleep, then as the sun sets, they rouse themselves and patrol their territory. They mark the trees in their area with urine and special scratches to deter rivals. Scent glands on their tail, paws, and face also leave smelly signals for any trespassing tigers.

Tigers travel many kilometres each night in search of food. Deer are their main prey, but they also hunt water buffalo, wild pigs, birds, fish, rats, and even frogs and lizards. The tiger's stripy coat helps it blend in with the shadows and soft toe pads muffle its footsteps as it stalks its prey. It creeps up very close, then attacks with a fatal pounce.

A large deer provides enough food for a week. Tigers drag their kill to a safe place before they begin to eat. When they are full, they hide their kill under leaves and dirt until they return for more.

WOW!
Every tiger's stripy coat is unique, like a fingerprint. One thing many tigers do have in common is a pattern that some say looks like the Chinese symbol for 'king' on their forehead.

FLOODED FOREST

Around 100 tigers live in the huge mangrove forest of the Sundarbans in West Bengal, India. Mangrove forests grow on tropical coasts where the tide washes over the land. The Sundarbans is criss-crossed with rivers and streams that flow into the ocean. The fresh water mingles with the salty sea, providing homes for a rich variety of wildlife. Sundarbans tigers spend time on the marshy land and in the water. They are excellent swimmers and cross wide rivers to reach their hunting grounds.

TREES

Mangroves are tough trees that can grow in hot, salty swamps. They stand on long, tangled roots that reach down into the water. The roots form a cage where crabs and small fish can hide. The thick mangroves also provide a natural barrier that protects the land beyond from tropical storms and flooding.

DEER

The chital, or spotted deer, is the tiger's main prey. Herds of deer browse on the lush leaves and forage for shellfish among the mangrove roots. They listen out for predators and, when they sense danger, they sound the alarm, stamping their hooves and letting out shrill calls. Without tigers to keep their numbers down, the deer would eat all the plants and small trees. The trees would struggle to regrow, which would change the forest and impact the other animals that live there.

LIZARD

A water monitor is a top hunter and a strong swimmer. It uses its tongue to sniff the air and detect its prey. It eats fish, crabs, frogs, snakes, insects, rodents, birds, and bird eggs.

FISH

Mudskippers are fish that can breathe in water and on land. At low tide, they use their front fins to 'walk' on the mud. They eat worms, insects, and shrimp.

CROCODILE

Saltwater crocodiles are the largest reptiles in the world. They lurk on riverbanks, with only their nostrils and eyes above the water. When unsuspecting prey pass by, a crocodile explodes out of the water, grabbing their victim in its powerful jaws. Fish, birds, wild boar, monkeys, and deer are all on the menu.

An arm for gathering food.

AFRICAN ELEPHANT

POWERFUL AND PROTECTIVE, CLEVER AND CARING

Scientific name: Loxodonta africana | **Lifespan in wild:** up to 70 years
Height: 3 m | **Weight:** up to 6,000 kg | **Location:** Southern and Eastern Africa

African savanna elephants are the biggest land animals on Earth. These plant-eating giants are strong enough to uproot a tree, but nimble enough to pluck a single berry from a bush. They are constantly on the move, roaming across the wide grasslands in search of food and water to satisfy their huge appetites.

A syringe for sucking up and squirting out water. It can hold up to 8 litres.

ZOOM IN!

The trunk is made up of more muscles than there are in the entire human body. As well as breathing and smelling, it used for all sorts of tasks.

FEEDING THE FAMILY

Elephants live in close family groups of 10 or more females and their calves. Males leave the group as soon as they are grown up. An older female, called a matriarch, is in charge of leading the herd, using her experience to guide them to fresh grazing grounds and watering holes.

Adult elephants can spend 18 hours each day grazing on leaves, grasses, twigs, bark, and fruit. They need to munch up to 150 kilograms of food each day – that's like 1,200 carrots!

Elephant calves are born hungry. Within 20 minutes they are able to stand and guzzle their mother's milk. They drink about 9 litres a day. After two days, calves can keep up with the herd, which keeps on moving in their search of the next meal.

WOW!
A newborn calf can weigh 120 kilograms – that's about the same as a refrigerator. Fully grown male elephants weigh around 6,000 kilograms – the same as three family cars.

GIVE AND TAKE ON THE SAVANNA

Savannas are vast areas of tropical grassland scattered with trees. They have a dry season and a wet season. Savanna elephants shape the landscape and help other plants and animals to thrive.

Elephants dig the watering holes that provide a source of water for many different animals, including ostrich, zebra, buffalo, giraffe, and gazelles. During the dry season, elephants dig into the soil with their tusks to uncover underground springs.

LIZARDS

As elephants march across the savanna, they leave a trail of damaged shrubs and trees in their wake. Small animals, like the dwarf gecko, use the nooks and crannies in the broken tree branches and torn bark to shelter from the heat and predators. The crevices also make a safe spot for lizards to lay their eggs.

DUNG BEETLES

Elephants eat a lot, so they poo a lot – up to 15 times a day! Dung beetles roll the poo into balls, relocate it, and bury it, making the soil more fertile. The dung balls contain seeds eaten by the elephants, which grow into new trees, shrubs, and grasses.

BIRDS

Oxpeckers land on elephants and other grazing animals to eat the lice and ticks out of their skin and hair. The elephants get the dangerous bugs removed and the oxpeckers get a free snack. Cattle egrets also perch on top of elephants, ready to swoop down and eat the insects stirred up by the elephant's feet as they walk through the grass.

BABOONS

In parts of central Africa, elephants have been seen to work closely with olive baboons. The elephants dig water holes that the baboons drink from. In return, the baboons alert the elephants to any approaching danger they spot from their treetop homes.

ECOTOURISM

Wildlife reserves are large, protected areas where animals can roam freely and be safely observed in the wild by visitors on safari. People from around the world are drawn to see elephants, rhinos, giraffes, and lions, but the reserves also protect the many other animals that live there.

Feather tip is stiff and oily to repel water.

Downy base traps heat next to the body.

ZOOM IN!
Special tightly packed feathers keep the penguins warm and dry. They use their beaks to coat their feathers with waterproof oil that comes from a gland at the base of their tail.

ADÉLIE PENGUIN

TINY BUT TOUGH, FEATHERY BUT FEISTY

Scientific name: Pygoscelis adeliae | **Lifespan in wild:** 11–20 years
Height: 70 cm | **Weight:** 3–6 kg | **Location:** Antarctica

Adélie penguins thrive in one of the world's harshest environments. These plucky birds spend three-quarters of their lives hunting in the icy sea. When threatened, they have been known to take on seals, large seabirds, and even visiting scientists.

BRINGING UP BABY

In the spring, Adélie penguins come in from the sea to find a mate and breed. They form colonies of up to a million pairs on the rocky coast.

Males build a nest to attract a female. They use their beaks to roll small stones into place. Some steal neighbours' stones in a bid to make the best nest! Females lay two eggs that hatch after about 35 days. The chicks emerge covered in fuzzy down. For the first three weeks the parents take turns to hunt and guard the chicks, then the young are left together in a 'crèche' while the adults hunt. They catch shrimp-like krill, which they regurgitate for the chicks.

After about nine weeks, the chicks have grown adult feathers and are ready to head out to sea. They will not return for at least three years, when they too will breed.

WOW!
Some years the sea is still frozen and penguins must waddle over 50 kilometres from their nests to reach the water.

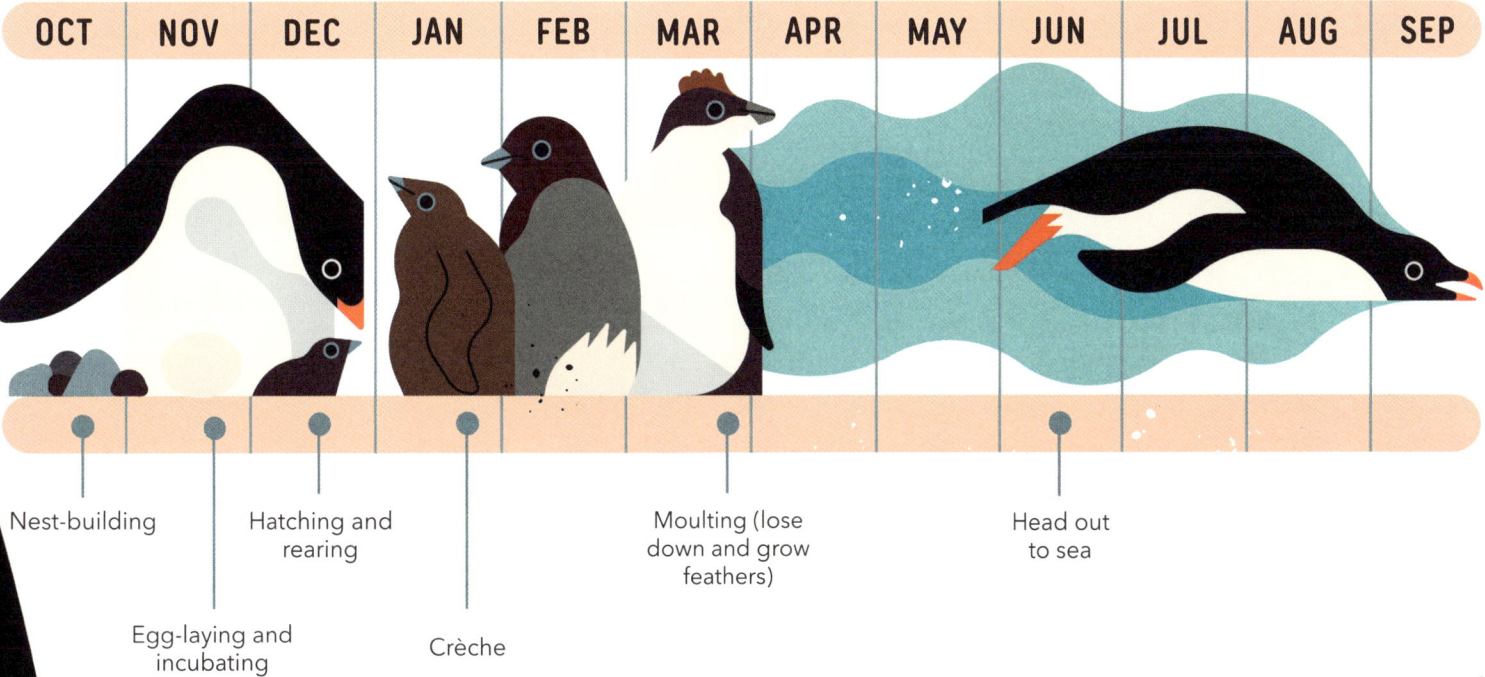

OCT	NOV	DEC	JAN	FEB	MAR	APR	MAY	JUN	JUL	AUG	SEP

Nest-building

Egg-laying and incubating

Hatching and rearing

Crèche

Moulting (lose down and grow feathers)

Head out to sea

KEEPING THE CLIMATE IN BALANCE

Antarctica is the coldest, windiest continent on Earth. It is also the largest desert. Not the hot, sandy sort, but an ice-covered wilderness where no trees or shrubs can grow. Although the land is empty, the ocean that surrounds Antarctica is bursting with life.

Ninety per cent of the fresh water on Earth is frozen at the top and bottom of the world. The polar ice caps reflect the Sun's rays, which keeps the planet's temperature just right. Global warming is slowly melting the ice caps, which means fewer rays are reflected.

KRILL

These small animals are the superfood that feeds everything from fish to giant whales. They eat tiny marine plants, called plankton, that grow under the ice. Millions of krill form super-swarms that can be seen from space.

SEALS

Seals eat fish, squid, or krill. The leopard seal will also hunt penguins and other seals.

WHALES

Baleen whales gulp giant mouthfuls of sea water and strain out the krill. Toothed whales hunt squid and fish. The orca is a top, toothed predator that hunts penguins, seals, and other whales.

PENGUINS

Penguins eat small fish and krill. An Adélie penguin eats about 1,200 krill a day!

BIRDS

In spring, over 100 million birds breed in Antarctica. Most feed on fish and krill, but skuas prey on Adélie eggs and young chicks.

ICE COOL

The Southern Ocean is a marine ecosystem where ice and water, sunlight and sea currents, plants and animals all play their part. Many birds and whales are seasonal visitors that come to feed and breed, but penguins and seals live in the cold all year round. Together, they make a giant living jigsaw that provides food for all.

25

SOLITARY BEES
HARMLESS AND HELPFUL, HARDWORKING HEROES

Scientific name: Andrena, Xylocopa, Osmia, Megachile | **Lifespan:** 11 months developing, 4–6 weeks as adults | **Length:** 5–17 mm | **Location:** Everywhere except Antarctica

Most of the world's 20,000 bee species are not the honey-making kind. In the UK, out of 270 different bee species, 25 are bumblebees and only one is a honeybee. All the rest are solitary. In the UK, there are four main types: mining, mason, leaf cutter, and carpenter bees. They come in many sizes, shapes, and colours, and they are all champion pollinators.

A single red mason bee can do the pollination work of 120 honeybees.

ZOOM IN!
Solitary bees are the best bee pollinators because they deposit so much pollen. They collect pollen all over their fuzzy legs and bodies, which brushes off when they land on a flower.

In the UK, solitary bees pollinate many of the crops we eat, including broccoli, cabbages, tomatoes, raspberries, as well as apples and orchard fruits.

BEE-ING ALONE

Where honeybees like to live together in a busy hive, as their name might suggest, solitary bees nest alone. Solitary bees mate in the spring and summer, then females get busy nest-building.

MASON BEES nest in plant stems or in walls. They use mud to line cavities in cracked brickwork and stone.

Mason and carpenter bees divide their tunnel nest into cells by building walls.

CARPENTER BEES nest in rotting wood. They drill round tunnels with their powerful jaws.

Mining and leafcutter bees dig a chamber for each egg in their underground burrow.

MINING BEES dig burrows in soil, grassy banks, and lawns.

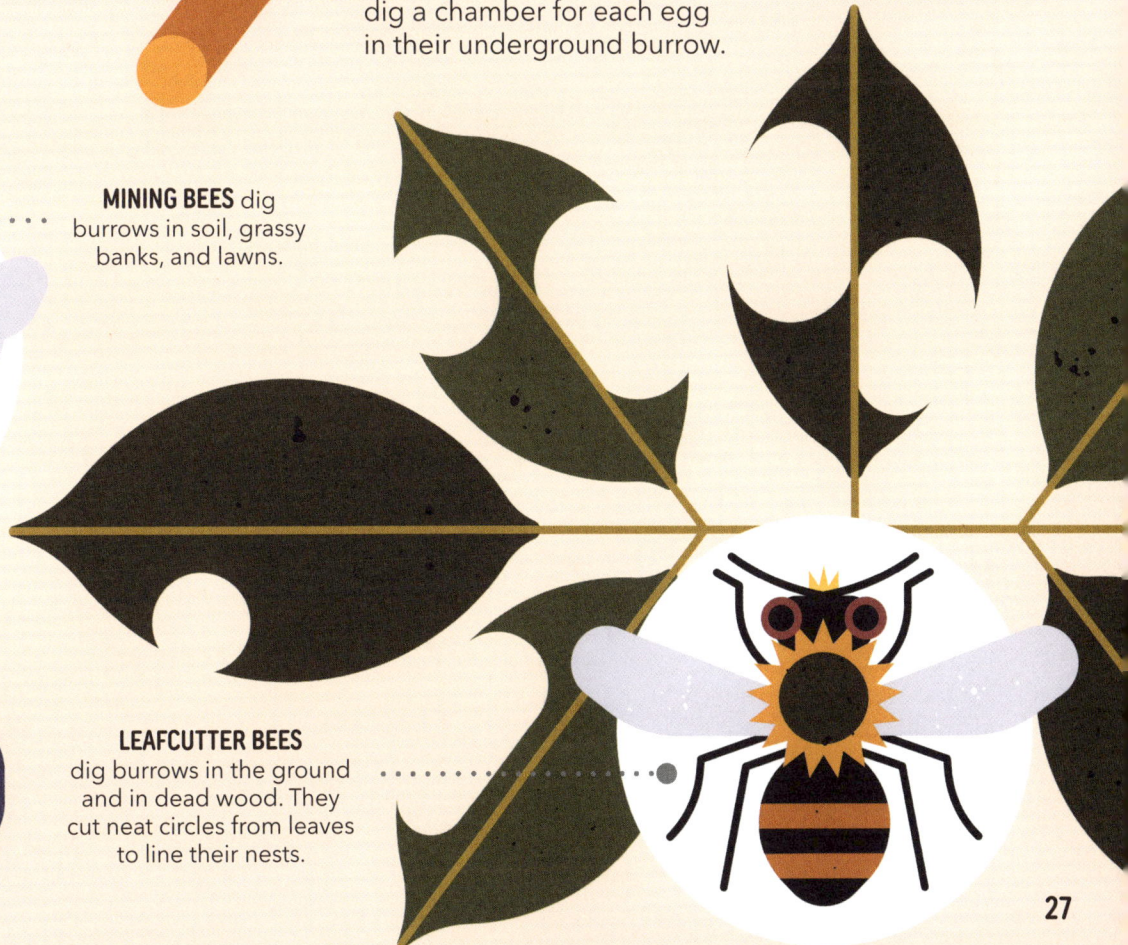

LEAFCUTTER BEES dig burrows in the ground and in dead wood. They cut neat circles from leaves to line their nests.

FOOD FROM FLOWERS

Solitary bees may be tiny, but they have a big impact on the environment. Our countryside, gardens, and green spaces would be far less colourful without them, and many wild animals would go hungry. In the spring and summer, bees buzz around blossoming shrubs, trees, and wildflowers. These pollinated plants then provide food and shelter for insects, birds, and mammals throughout the year.

WILD FLOWERS

In the spring and early summer, meadows and hedgerows burst into life. Wild flowers provide pollen and nectar for bees and other pollinators, including butterflies, moths, and beetles. Pollination ensures that the flowers will bloom again the following season.

HEDGEHOGS

These spiky mammals come out of hibernation in the spring. They hide in the shady undergrowth during the day and head out at sunset to hunt for bugs. Like a prickly pest control, they gobble slugs and caterpillars that munch on new shoots and leaves.

BUTTERFLIES

As the weather warms up, butterflies feed on nectar and lay their eggs on fresh, juicy leaves. The caterpillars hatch and consume the leafy banquet. Both butterflies and their caterpillars are preyed upon by many birds.

BATS

Many kinds of bats, including the barbastelle bat and brown long-eared bat, roost in tree holes in woodlands. They hunt at night, flitting between the trees to snap up moths and flying insects. They catch and eat them in mid-air.

BIRDS

From late summer, through autumn and into winter, the trees and shrubs that were visited by bees earlier in the year are laden with fruit. Birds such as blackbirds, robins, thrushes, and woodpeckers feed on the berries. In winter, the holly and ivy berries provide a festive feast.

SQUIRRELS

In the winter, squirrels dig up the stores of food that they buried in the autumn. Their cache of acorns, hazelnuts, chestnuts, and beech nuts provide them with food during the cold months.

DEER

In autumn, fallow deer, red deer, and roe deer browse among the woods searching for sweet chestnuts and acorns. These high-energy nuts are packed with carbohydrates and fat that help the deer put on weight in the run-up to winter.

HAWKSBILL TURTLE

ANCIENT AND AWESOME, HELPFUL AND HUNTED

Scientific name: Eretmochelys imbricata | **Lifespan in wild:** 30-50 years | **Length:** 75-115 cm
Weight: 40-70 kg | **Location:** Tropical waters of Atlantic, Pacific, and Indian Oceans

The hawksbill turtle is named after its narrow, beak-like mouth, which is used for reaching food in narrow cracks and crevices. Hawksbills glide gracefully through crystal-clear waters, visiting colourful coral reefs and tropical beaches. Although it sounds idyllic, these gentle creatures face many dangers over their long lives.

ZOOM IN!

A turtle's shell is covered in scutes – hard, scale-like plates. Each scute is covered in a unique pattern of amber, yellow, brown, and black, which help the turtle to blend in with coral reefs and rocky seabeds.

OCEAN TRAVELLERS

Hawksbill turtles are found throughout the tropical waters of the Atlantic, Pacific, and Indian Oceans. Like other sea turtles, they make incredible migrations, criss-crossing oceans and travelling thousands of kilometres in their lifetime.

JUVENILE MIGRATIONS

After hatching, turtles move to the open sea, where they drift for one to five years. Juveniles then migrate to coastal areas to feed and grow into adults.

FORAGING MIGRATIONS

Adult hawksbills journey to feeding grounds, such as coral reefs, where they spend most of their time.

NESTING MIGRATIONS

Every two to five years, male and female adults migrate to their breeding grounds. Their journeys can range from few hundred kilometres to over a thousand kilometres. The turtles are driven by their instinct to mate and lay their eggs in the place where they hatched decades earlier.

HUNDREDS OF HATCHLINGS

Females nest on small, sheltered beaches. They crawl ashore at night to lay their eggs above the tide line.

They dig a pit with their flippers, lay 130 to 160 golf-ball-sized eggs, then cover them with warm sand.

WOW!

The temperature of the nest determines the gender of the hatchlings. Hotter temperatures produce more females. Due to global warming, the number of female turtles is increasing.

After about two months, the hatchlings emerge. They are a few inches long with heart-shaped shells.

The hatchlings head towards the bright horizon where they know the ocean lies.

Only one in every thousand hatchlings survives to adulthood.

REEF HEROES AND VILLAINS

Australia's Great Barrier Reef stretches for over 2,300 kilometres. It formed slowly over thousands of years and provides food and shelter to an incredible number of marine plants and animals.

Some creatures spend their lives on the reef, while others visit to breed and hunt. Hawksbill turtles are important residents that feed on shellfish, sea urchins, jellyfish, and their favourite food – sponges. By eating sponges, Hawksbills help to keep the reef healthy. They create space for slow-growing coral to thrive, which gives reef fish better access to the coral.

SPONGES

The Great Barrier Reef is home to at least 2,500 species of sponges. Sponges are an animal, not a plant. A healthy reef needs about 10 per cent of its surface to be covered by sponges. They protect coral from extreme temperatures and bright sunlight. However, if the number of hawksbill turtles drops, the number of sponges quickly grows.

CORAL

Corals are made up of thousands of tiny animals, called polyps, that have a hard, external skeleton. They form colourful structures with ridges and crevices that give shelter to marine life. Coral reefs protect coastal areas by reducing the power of waves hitting the shore. They also shield mangrove forests and seagrass beds that act as nurseries for many marine animals.

CROWN-OF-THORNS STARFISH

This large starfish is covered in venomous spines that are harmful to humans and many fish. It also devours coral. When too many starfish gather in one area, they can quickly destroy large areas of reef.

HUMPHEAD WRASSE

These enormous fish can grow to over 1.8 metres long and live to be over 30 years old. They roam coral reefs in search of prey such as snails, clams, crabs, and starfish, including the crown-of-thorns starfish. They help to control the number of this coral-eating reef predator.

GIANT CLAM

A giant clam can live for up to 100 years. It feeds by drawing in water through a large opening and sifting out plankton to eat. Giant clams act like water filters, helping to keep the reefs waters clear and clean.

BLUE TANG

These dazzling fish rest and hide from predators in the coral's nooks. They are important because they feed on algae and seaweed, which can smother the coral reef if they grow out of control.

33

PACIFIC SALMON

SLEEK AND STRONG, TRAVELLERS AND TRANSFORMERS

Scientific name: Oncorhynchus | **Lifespan in wild:** 2–7 years | **Length:** 45–76 cm
Weight: 1.3–57 kg | **Location:** North Pacific waters of Canada, Japan, Russia, and the USA

Pacific salmon make one of the world's most epic journeys. They travel from gentle streams, lakes, and rivers to the wild and salty Pacific Ocean – then back again. Some salmon swim for over 3,000 kilometres to return to the place where they hatched. Their trip is fraught with danger. Those that survive, complete their mission to start the next generation of salmon.

SMOLTS

FRY

ALEVIN

THE CIRCLE OF LIFE

There are five species of Pacific salmon in the USA and Canada: chinook, coho, chum, pink, and sockeye. They are all adapted to survive in fresh and salty water.

HATCHING AND HIDING

When they hatch in fresh water, they are called 'alevin'. These tiny fish have an orange sack of yolk on their belly leftover from their egg. The yolk nourishes the fish for the first weeks of their life. They hide on the gravelly riverbed and grow. Once they begin to swim, they are called 'fry'. They develop markings to help them blend in and hide from predators.

CHANGING AND GROWING

The young salmon, known as 'smolts', develop a silvery coating over their scales to protect them as they begin their long journey from fresh water to the salty ocean. The fish grow into adult salmon in the North Pacific Ocean. They spend between one and six years feeding on small fish, squid, shrimp, and eels.

RETURNING AND REPRODUCING

Salmon know instinctively when to return home. They battle strong currents as they swim upstream. They leap up waterfalls and rapids, and many fall prey to hungry predators such as bears, eagles, and wolves. Their incredible sense of smell leads them back to the exact place where they hatched. Now the salmon spawn. Females release their eggs and the males fertilize them. Soon after, the salmon die.

ZOOM IN!
When they return to fresh water to spawn, the male sockeye salmon undergoes physical changes. Their mouths curve upwards and they grow large teeth, which they use to fight off rival males. They also develop a hump on their back.

ADULT SALMON

LIFE AND DEATH IN ALASKA

Many types of salmon are considered keystone species. This means that they are so important that without them, an ecosystem would change dramatically or could even cease to exist.

Sockeye salmon are a keystone species in the marine ecosystem of Bristol Bay in southwest Alaska. As well as four other types of Pacific salmon, up to 40 million sockeye salmon swarm into the network of streams, rivers, and lakes in spring and summer. Their bodies are rich with nutrients from the ocean. As they swim upstream, they provide valuable food for all sorts of wildlife

BEARS

The Bristol Bay area is home to around 10,000 brown bears. They spend the winter hibernating, then emerge in the spring, ravenous and ready to feast on the returning salmon. Bears line the rivers ready to snap up the fish as they leap up the rapids.

BALD EAGLES

There are more bald eagles in Alaska than in the whole of the rest of the USA. These powerful hunters soar high above the water. Their sharp eyes can spot fish from over a kilometre away. They swoop down at 160 kilometres an hour and snatch up salmon in their sharp talons.

WOLVERINES

These top scavengers have a keen sense of smell. They sniff out remains left behind by bigger predators, like bears and wolves. If they are lucky there will be a moose carcass, but they will steal bird eggs, eagle chicks, or scoop salmon out of the shallows.

MOOSE

Moose do not eat salmon, but they still benefit from their return. Rotting salmon carcasses break down and fertilize the soil of the surrounding riverbanks. The lush mosses, herbs, shrubs, and trees that grow contain the nutrients from the salmon, which are eaten by moose and other grazing animals.

FLIES

Flies lay their eggs in salmon carcasses that wash up on the shores. The larvae hatch and feast on the fish. These same insects will end up becoming food for the new generation of salmon waiting to hatch beneath the gravel.

GREY WOLF
SOCIABLE AND SMART, NOISY BUT STEALTHY

Scientific name: Canis lupus | Lifespan in wild: 6-8 years | Height: 65-90 cm
Length: 100-180 cm | Weight: 18-80 kg | Location: Canada, North America,
Asia, Russia, Central and Eastern Europe

Grey wolves used to roam wild all over the northern half of the world. They thrive wherever there is plenty of prey, from snowy mountains and open plains to dense forests. Horror films and fairy tales paint wolves as savage and greedy, but we are more of a threat to wolves than they are to us.

Wide paws spread the wolf's weight.

Skin stretched between the toes, called webbing, stops wolves from sinking into soft snow.

Their long claws are for digging and gripping the earth while running, not for grabbing prey.

ZOOM IN!
A wolf's large paws are perfectly adapted to help it travel long distances and chase down prey over rough terrain.

TOP DOGS

Yellowstone National Park in the USA is a wilderness with over 60 different mammals, including bears, bison, elk, coyotes, and cougars. Today there are also wolves in the park, but in the past they were seen as a danger to people and livestock, and hunted until there were none left. Wolves were brought back to Yellowstone when people realized that these top predators are essential to the ecosystem.

Grey wolves live in family packs led by two alpha dogs – an older male and female. Working as a team, the pack captures large animals, such as elk, bison, and deer, defends their territory, and shares the care of young or sick pack members.

Wolves have excellent night vision, sharp hearing, and an incredible sense of smell, which all help them to catch their prey. They howl to warn of danger, to fend off rival wolves and to keep pack members together. Each wolf has a unique howl and the sound can carry up to 16 kilometres.

WOW!
When a pack of wolves howls together, they harmonize on different notes. This makes it sound like there are more of them.

WOLVES CHANGE RIVERS

If a key predator is removed from an ecosystem, it upsets the natural balance. When the last wolf pups were killed by rangers in the 1920s, Yellowstone was left without its top hunter. Over the next 100 years their absence caused ripples of change that affected every living thing, from elk, beavers, and birds, to bugs, fish, plants, and trees.

In 1995, fourteen wild wolves were captured in Canada and released into the park. Over the last 30 years, their numbers have grown and today there are 10 wolf packs hunting in Yellowstone. Their arrival put all of the negative changes into reverse and, slowly but surely, the natural balance was restored.

ELK

Without wolves, the elk lost their main predator and the herds grew in size. They no longer needed to take cover among the trees, but grazed happily in the grassy meadows. They gobbled shrubs and grasses and browsed on young trees. With no wolves around, elk spent longer drinking from the rivers. They broke down the banks with their hooves and muddied the waters.

BEAVERS

Beavers eat trees to survive the winter. They also fell young trees to build dams across rivers and streams. Dams slow the water's flow, creating pools and shady shallows where fish, frogs, reptiles, and otters nest and feed. With elk browsing on riverbanks, there was not enough food for the beavers and their numbers fell. When beavers disappeared, so did the river life.

BIRDS AND BEES

The hungry elk herds eventually led to fewer plants and trees growing along riverbanks. This meant there were not enough nesting sites for birds such as warblers, fly-catchers, and song birds. Pollinating insects, bees, and hummingbirds had fewer flowers to feed on, which meant that blossoming plants and trees did not make fruit, berries, nuts, and seeds – important foods for bears and small mammals.

SCAVENGERS

Many Yellowstone animals benefit from scraps left by predators. In the spring, grizzly and black bears emerge from their hibernation, ready for an easy meal. Ravens, eagles, and magpies wait for their chance to pick the bones. Even beetles and bugs feed on the wolves' leftovers. Without the wolves, there were far fewer elk carcasses to feed scavengers.

PEOPLE

The return of the wolves benefitted people as well as wildlife. Millions of visitors travel to Yellowstone each year, and hundreds of thousands of them go to see the wolves. This brings money to the local community and secures jobs for people working in the park and the tourist industry. Local residents even have cleaner drinking water now.

ZOOM IN!
Some adult male orangutans have flanges – prominent cheek pads that develop when they are about 35 years old. Flanges are a sign of maturity and can help attract mates.

ORANGUTANS

SMART AND SKILFUL, GENTLE GYMNASTS

Scientific name: Pongo | **Lifespan in wild:** 30–50 years | **Weight:** 35 kg (females), 85 kg (males) | **Height:** 115–150 cm | **Location:** Sumatra (Indonesia) and Borneo (Malaysia and Indonesia)

Orangutans are known for their shaggy, red fur and friendly, intelligent faces. Their name means 'man of the forest' and they spend almost all of their lives high up in the rainforest trees, searching for fruit, sleeping, and swinging from branch to branch.

TREETOP LIVING

Orangutans are amazing acrobats. They have long, strong arms and grasping hands much like ours. Their feet are also like hands and are used for gripping and climbing.

Orangutans are clever and nimble-fingered. They make tools from plants. Big leaves make handy umbrellas, small leaves make a glove for holding prickly fruit. A stick can be a dipper for scooping up ants or a rod for grabbing hard-to-reach fruit.

Every night, orangutans weave together supple branches to make a treetop nest to sleep in. In wet weather, they sometimes add a roof.

Unlike other great apes, adults spend most of their time alone, but mothers care for their young until they are at least seven years old. Babies cling on tightly as they are taken for a swing through the trees. Mums show youngsters which leaves, flowers, fruits, and insects are good to eat.

WOW!
Orangutans' arms stretch to their ankles when they are standing. Males' arms measure over 2 metres from tip to tip – that's as wide as a giraffe's neck is long.

GARDENERS OF THE FOREST

Borneo is home to the greatest number of wild orangutans. As they roam through the treetops, they munch upon up to 500 different types of plant, but orangutans are gardeners as well as guzzlers. Undigested fruit seeds pass out in the orangutans' poo. The seeds take root on the forest floor and new trees grow. This keeps the forests healthy for orangutans and the thousands of other animal species that share their leafy home – many of which are endangered and found nowhere else on Earth.

SQUIRRELS

Borneo's dense forests are home to many species of squirrel, from the mouse-sized pygmy squirrel to the giant squirrel. There are flying squirrels, too. Skin between their front and back legs acts like wings. When they stretch out their limbs, they can glide between the trees.

PROBOSCIS MONKEY

Male proboscis monkeys have unusually large noses. This huge fleshy snout is used to attract a mate! Scientists believe it may also boost the honks and snorts the monkeys make to impress females and intimidate rivals.

SLOW LORIS

These small primates have huge, round eyes to help them hunt at night. Occasionally, when there is not much ripe fruit, orangutans eat slow loris, but they have to be careful – these cute creatures have a poisonous bite!

BORNEAN ELEPHANT

Meet the largest mammal on the island of Borneo. These gentle, playful elephants are shorter and chunkier than their Indian cousins. They have shorter trunks and a smaller, rounder face too, but longer tails that can reach to the ground.

HORNBILLS

Borneo is home to eight types of hornbill. They have a long, curved beak topped with a hollow, bony structure called a 'casque'. The casque acts like a megaphone for blasting out the bird's calls.

SUMATRAN RHINOCEROS

Like the orangutan, this small, endangered rhino only survives on the islands of Sumatra and Borneo. It is covered in patches of short, stiff hair. The hair helps mud stick to its skin, keeping it cool.

WOW!

Sixty per cent of the food orangutans eat is fruit. Their favourite is the spiky durian fruit, which is said to smell like rotting flesh and smelly socks!

JAGUAR

STEALTHY AND PATIENT, AGILE AND DEADLY

Scientific name: Panthera onca | **Lifespan in wild:** 12–15 years | **Length:** up to 240 cm nose to tail
Weight: 55–95 kg | **Location:** Latin America, from Mexico to Argentina

No prey is too big for the mighty jaguar. This skilful hunter can be found prowling along riverbanks, wading through swamps, or waiting patiently in the undergrowth. When it sees its chance, it is all over in a flash of orange and black and a bone-crushing bite.

The blotches break up the cat's shape and create a dappled effect that matches the patches of light and shade in the tropical forest.

ZOOM IN!

Apart from their faces, Jaguars aren't spotty – they are covered in flowers! The rings of black patches on their fur are known as 'rosettes', because they look like rose petals.

GRABBING A BITE

Jaguars hunt alone, often travelling long distances in search of food. They hide in the shadows, preying on anything that comes their way, including deer, monkeys, capybaras, armadillos, and iguanas. Jaguars are strong swimmers, so they also catch fish, turtles, and caimans in rivers and lakes.

This cat does not chase down prey, but stalks it silently. Once the jaguar comes within striking distance, it launches a deadly attack. The name jaguar comes from the Tipi-Guarani word 'yaguar', meaning 'he who kills with one leap', and that is all it takes.

For their size, jaguars have the most powerful bite of any big cat. They can sink their teeth through thick caiman skin and hard turtle shell, as well as crunching through solid bone. Their wide jaws and mighty bite mean they can take down animals up to four times their own weight.

WOW!
The jaguar's roar is often called a 'saw' because it sounds like wood being sawed in one direction.

47

INTO THE AMAZON

Over 70 per cent of the world's wild jaguars are found in the Amazon Rainforest. The dense forest stretches for millions of kilometres and is home to hundreds of thousands of different species of plant and animal. The jaguar is the number one terrestrial predator amongst them. This elusive meat-eater needs to hunt over a large area to catch enough to eat. It plays an important part in keeping nature in balance in the Amazon.

FISH

The Amazon River teems with fish. Piranhas have razor-sharp teeth, but they mostly eat seeds, insects, and small fish. Pirarucu are the river's fierce hunters and are one of the world's largest freshwater fish. They mostly eat other fish, but are known to leap out of the water to grab small birds and lizards from low-hanging branches.

FROGS

Over 400 species of frog and toad are found in the damp rainforest. The most eye-catching are tiny poison dart frogs. They are some of the most brightly coloured and toxic creatures on Earth. Their dazzling skin warns other animals to beware.

BLACK CAIMAN

This powerful predator is related to the alligator. It lurks in the muddy waters, waiting to snap up a fish or a turtle. It will also take a capybara or a tapir that ventures too close. Caimans can be hunted by jaguars.

TAPIR

The tapir has a nose like a short trunk that it uses to pluck fruit and strip leaves from branches. Although it looks like a pig, it is related to horses and rhinos. Tapir live in the forest, but cool off in the water and dive down to eat river plants.

ANACONDA

These huge snakes can be as long as a bus. They are slow-moving on land, but stealthy in water. They use their powerful jaws to hold on to their prey while they squeeze them to death with their muscular bodies. Anacondas unhinge their jaws and swallow their kill whole.

CAPYBARA

Meet the world's largest rodent. It wallows in rivers, lakes, and swamps and eats the plants and grasses that grow at the water's edge. When threatened, capybara can hide under water, holding their breath for over four minutes.

SCIMITAR-HORNED ORYX

ELEGANT BUT HARDY, ANCIENT BUT ENDANGERED

Scientific name: Oryx dammah | **Lifespan in wild:** 15–20 years | **Height:** 120–140 cm
Weight: 140 kg (females), 210 kg (males) | **Location:** Sahara and Sahel, North Africa

Scimitar-horned oryx look like mythical creatures with their white coats, heart-shaped faces, and slender horns, but life is no fairy tale for these elegant antelope. They survive in one of the hottest, driest places on the planet.

ZOOM IN!

This species of oryx is named after a curved Arabian sword called a scimitar. Like the sword, the antelope's sharp-tipped horns can be a fearsome deterrent or a lethal weapon. When threatened, an oryx will attack, using its horns like spears. They have been known to kill lions!

The horns can measure over 130 centimetres.

SURVIVING IN THE SAHARA

These hardy antelope are perfectly suited to life in a hot, dry habitat. They travel long distances across the dusty landscape searching for plants to graze on. Their wide, splayed hooves spread their weight, allowing them to walk without sinking into the soft sand. Their cream-coloured coats reflect the Sun's strong rays, and their thick eyelashes protect them from sand whipped up by the wind.

There is very little water, but oryx can go for months without drinking. They get all the moisture they need from the plants they eat. They graze on desert grasses during the rainy season, and browse on leaves, roots, and buds during the dry season. Their favourite food, wild melon, gives them plenty of liquid.

Oryx graze at dawn and dusk when the Sun is at its lowest, and seek out patches of shade during the blistering heat of the day. They scrape away the hot sand with their hooves to create a cool bed to lie on.

DESERT DWELLERS

Scimitar-horned onyx are important to the ecosystem of the Sahel – a dry region that lies between lush grasslands and the vast, scorching Sahara Desert. The antelope browse on the thorny vegetation, helping to keep it from becoming overgrown. Oryx are also vital prey for predators, such as lions, hyenas, and wild dogs, in a place where food is scarce.

A century ago, thousands of scimitar-horned oryx roamed across the Sahel. Over the years, they faced threats from human hunters, and herds of cattle ate the oryxs' food. Then droughts and swarms of locusts stripped the land of plants. By the year 2000, the oryx were extinct in the wild. Zoos around the world worked together to breed captive oryx. In 2017, fourteen animals were released in Chad. Today at least 500 oryx roam wild once more.

DESERT LOCUST

They look like large grasshoppers, but desert locusts are much more destructive. After heavy rains, they can multiply quickly and form swarms of up to 80 million insects. They fly hundreds of kilometres a day, devouring every leaf, bud, and stem in sight.

NORTH AFRICAN OSTRICH

The ostrich is the world's biggest bird. It is too heavy to fly, but it can sprint up to 72 kilometres per hour on its long, powerful legs. It has a sharp claw on each foot and can deliver a dangerous kick when threatened.

RUPPELL'S VULTURE

This large scavenger does an important job of cleaning up after predators. It soars high above the land, searching for meaty remains. When it spies a carcass, it swoops down and picks the bones clean.

DAMA GAZELLE

Herds of nimble dama gazelle are constantly on the move, searching for food and water. They stand on their hind legs to nibble the leaves on shrubs and thorny bushes. Hyenas, cheetahs, and wild dogs prey on gazelles, but the gazelles get some protection from the herd with its many watchful eyes.

DESERT HORNED VIPER

This snake gets its name from the pointed scale above each eye. It moves quickly across the loose sand by sidewinding – throwing its body forwards and leaving a sideways trail of curved tracks. It ambushes prey by covering itself in sand, then striking suddenly, injecting venom with its sharp fangs.

AFRICAN WILD DOG

The large, rounded ears of the African wild dog swivel like radars, picking up faint sounds in the distance. They are ruthless and organized hunters, but they are also sociable and playful. They care for the old, sick, and less able dogs in the pack.

SPOTTED HYENA

Spotted hyenas are happy to dine on others' scraps, but their speed, sharp eyesight, and acute hearing make them excellent hunters, too. Packs work as a team to take down large prey such as antelope. They also hunt birds, lizards, and snakes.

GIANT PANDA
SOLITARY AND STRONG, SLEEPY AND SLOW

Scientific name: Ailuropoda melanoleuca | **Lifespan in wild:** 14–20 years
Height: 60–90 cm | **Length:** 150 cm | **Weight:** 75–125 kg | **Location:** Southwest China

The giant panda is adored around the world, but this distinctive bear only roams wild in a few areas of China. It is perfectly adapted to its mountain home, eating the local food and blending into its surroundings of dark forest or snowy slopes with its black-and-white colour scheme.

ZOOM IN!
Scientists believe pandas may recognize one another by the size and shape of their eye patches. Studies also show that their eye markings could be a warning. Pandas can make their patches look bigger when staring at a rival.

Most bears have round pupils, but pandas' pupils are vertical slits, like cats' eyes.

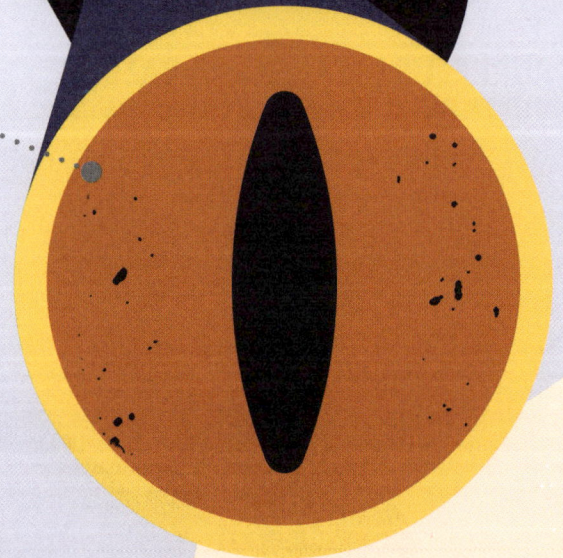

A QUIET LIFE

A panda's whole life revolves around bamboo. The stems, leaves, and shoots of this giant, woody grass make up 99 per cent of its diet. Pandas need to eat a lot of bamboo to get the nutrition they need, so they spend 10 to 16 hours a day foraging and feeding. They use their powerful jaws and wide, flat teeth to crush and grind through 12 to 38 kilograms of bamboo each day. They grip bamboo stems between their five fingers and a long wrist bone that sticks out like a fleshy thumb.

PASING THE TIME

Pandas do not hibernate like other bears because there is plenty of bamboo to eat all year round. Between eating, they spend time napping, but they are also good tree climbers and strong swimmers.

MEETING UP

Pandas live most of their life alone. They communicate with other pandas by rubbing their scent against tree trunks and rocks as they amble around their territory. Males and females meet briefly to mate during breeding season, then go their separate ways.

WOW!
Bamboo is so tough that panda poo contains lots of undigested bamboo bits. They poo more than 40 times a day. They even poo when they sleep!

MISTY MOUNTAINS

Most wild pandas live on the forested slopes of the Minshan and Qinling mountains in southwest China. Winters are long and the summers are short. Heavy rain falls all year round and the mountains are often shrouded in mist and cloud. A dense layer of lush bamboo grows beneath the trees. The pandas share their leafy home with some rare and colourful wildlife.

LEOPARDS

Giant pandas do not have many enemies, but snow leopards and clouded leopards sometimes prey upon their cubs.

RED PANDAS

Like the giant panda, these small tree-dwelling animals eat bamboo. The name panda is said to come from the Nepali word 'ponya', which means bamboo or plant-eating animal. Red pandas keep warm by wrapping their bushy tail around their body.

TAKIN

These shaggy mammals are related to sheep. They can leap nimbly from rock to rock, using their special split hooves to help them grip the steep slopes.

MONKEYS

A thick, golden coat helps the snub-nosed monkey survive in the cold climate. At night, groups of monkeys huddle together for warmth. They are preyed upon by eagles, wolves, and leopards.

PHEASANTS

A variety of brightly coloured pheasants forage for moss, seeds, berries, ferns, and shoots on the forest floor. They fly up into the trees to roost at night, safe from hungry predators.

CONSERVATION WORKS!

Today, the giant panda is loved throughout the world, but it was once among the most endangered mammals on Earth. Without conservation work, these iconic black-and-white bears could have been lost for good.

PEOPLE V. PANDAS

There were many threats to pandas' survival. Most of them were due to human activity.

HABITAT LOSS

As China's population grew, towns and cities spread into the pandas' habitat. Land was cleared for farming and building, and pandas were forced up into the mountains. Roads and railways cut across the pandas' ranges, and stretches of forest were chopped down for timber and firewood. Eventually the pandas were just left with patches of forest spread out across the mountains.

LACK OF FOOD

Bamboo plants die off every 40 to 120 years and it takes many years for them to regrow. The pandas' mountain ranges had fewer species of bamboo, so when one variety died off in the 1980s, there was not enough food for them to eat.

SHRINKING POPULATION

In the wild, giant pandas reproduce slowly. They usually give birth to one cub every few years. As the pandas' territory was broken up, it became harder for females to find a mate so fewer cubs were born.

POACHING AND HUNTING

In the 1980s, the illegal hunting of giant pandas was a big problem. They were caught and killed for their fur, which could fetch a high price.

HISTORIC GIANT PANDA HABITAT
CURRENT GIANT PANDA HABITAT

PROTECTING PANDAS

The Chinese government have worked with the World Wildlife Fund for decades to save their treasured national animal.

HABITAT PROTECTION

In the 1960s, the first four panda reserves were created. Today there are 67 reserves patrolled by trained rangers. Green corridors have been set up to allow pandas to roam safely to new areas, find food, and meet mates. Protecting pandas in this way also protects other threatened animals that share their habitat.

BREEDING AND RELEASING

Chengdu Panda Base was set up in 1987 to care for six starving giant pandas that had been rescued from the wild. Since then over 150 baby pandas have been born at the base. More research centres have been set up to breed pandas and release captive pandas into the wild.

LAWS AND PUNISHMENTS

In 1988, the Chinese government passed the Wildlife Protection Law to protect endangered animals. Since then, hunting and logging has been banned, and poachers have been caught and punished.

In 1988 there were just 1,114 giant pandas left in the wild, and in 1990 they were declared an endangered species. Today there are over 1,800 and their numbers are growing steadily.

The pandas' success story has shown that conservation really works and can help other endangered species. The pandas' plight has also made people aware of the threats facing wild animals and their habitats around the world.

GLOSSARY

ADAPTED
When a living thing is able to live in an environment because of changes that have happened to it over time, it has adapted.

ALGAE
Small plants that live in or near water and do not have ordinary leaves, stems, or roots.

BLUBBER
A thick layer of fat under the skin of sea mammals such as seals and whales that keeps them warm.

BREED
When animals mate and produce young.

CARCASS
The body of a large, dead animal.

COLONY
A group of the same type of animals, insects, or plants that live together.

DOWN
A covering of soft, fluffy feathers.

FERTILIZE

Egg: When a male animal fertilizes an egg with its sperm, a new young animal can develop.
Soil: When a substance is added to soil that helps plants to grow.

HIBERNATE

When animals spend the winter sleeping, they are hibernating. They come out of hibernation when they become active again.

INCUBATE

When a bird incubates its eggs, it keeps them warm until the young are ready to hatch.

LARVA (PLURAL: LARVAE)

A form of insect or animal that has left its egg but has not yet developed into an adult.

MAMMAL

Any animal that feeds on its mother's own milk when it is young. Most mammals do not lay eggs, but give birth to live young.

MARINE

Anything that is produced by, lives in, or grows in the sea.

MIGRATION

When an animal moves from one location or habitat to another, it migrates. It does this in order to breed or find food.

NECTAR

A sweet liquid made by flowers that is collected by bees and other insects as food.

NUTRIENT

A substance that is needed by plants and animals in order to live and grow.

POLLINATE

Some insects, birds, and animals take pollen from one plant to another so that new plant seeds can be produced. They are called pollinators.

PREDATOR

An animal that hunts, kills, and eats other animals.

PREY

An animal that is hunted, killed, and eaten by another animal.

PRIMATE

A type of mammal, which includes humans, monkeys, and apes.

REPTILE

A group of cold-blooded animals that have skins covered with hard scales and lay eggs.

RODENT

Small mammals that have sharp front teeth for gnawing. Rats, mice, and squirrels are rodents.

SPAWN

When fish or animals such as frogs lay their eggs.

SPECIES

A set of animals that have similar characteristics and can breed with each other. Tigers are a species and elephants are another.

TERRESTRIAL

A terrestrial animal lives on land or in the ground rather than in trees, in the air, or in the sea.

DK | Penguin Random House

Acquisitions Project Editor Sara Forster
Art Editor Chris Gould
Production Editor Siu Yin Chan
Production Controller Louise Minihane
Senior Acquisitions Editor Katy Flint
Managing Art Editor Vicky Short
Art Director Charlotte Coulais
Publishing Director Mark Searle

Designed by Sophie Gordon
Text by Catherine Ard
Artwork copyright © Owen Davey, 2025

First published in Great Britain in 2025 by
Dorling Kindersley Limited
20 Vauxhall Bridge Road,
London SW1V 2SA

Published by Dorling Kindersley Ltd in association with WWF.
WWF-UK is a registered charity in England and Wales 1081247
and in Scotland SC039593 and a company limited by
guarantee registered in England and Wales 4016725.

The authorised representative in the EEA is
Dorling Kindersley Verlag GmbH, Arnulfstr. 124,
80636 Munich, Germany

Page design copyright © 2025 Dorling Kindersley Limited
A Penguin Random House Company
10 9 8 7 6 5 4 3 2 1
001–348439–Jul/25

A CIP catalogue record for this book
is available from the British Library.
ISBN: 978-0-2417-2941-0

Printed and bound in Slovakia

www.dk.com